Susan L.

A to Z

OBJECT TALKS

26

That Teach About
—the—
Old Testament
for
Ages 6-12

Memorable Messages Your Kids Will Love!

STANDARD PUBLISHING

Cincinnati, Ohio

Dedication

*Then he opened their minds
so they could understand the Scriptures.*
Luke 24:45

CONTENTS

INTRODUCTION

How many days were in the Hebrew calendar?
What was the best way to swaddle a baby?
How did the Israelites clean their clothes?
When was the best time to wear a prayer shawl?

The answers from A to Z are found in *A to Z Object Talks That Teach About the Old Testament!* Kids will love making Hebrew soap as they learn about honoring God. They'll be high-stepping in their Super Sandals as they discover the importance of taking God's love around the world. And kids will understand the tradition of swaddling as they make Swaddling Bracelets and learn how God's love is wrapped around us. *A to Z Object Talks That Teach About the Old Testament* combines life-changing Bible truths with tons of cool Old Testament trivia that brings the Old Testament awesomely alive and makes it relevant for kids today.

Each memorable message in *A to Z Object Talks That Teach About the Old Testament* introduces an important biblical theme such as God's grace, obedience, fueling our faith, and honoring God. Kids interact with each message by reading from the Bible, discussing the importance of each theme, and making cool crafts or super snacks as reminders of the Old Testament and its powerful Bible truths. Kids come away from these meaningful messages filled with

- **powerful reminders of God's Word,**
- **an appreciation for the Old Testament,**
- **fascinating facts and too-cool Bible trivia, and**
- **a sense of community and teamwork.**

Use these motivating object talks as mini lessons on Old Testament truths, as cool, stand-alone object talks or kids' sermons, or as powerful Bible-story enrichment tools. Make every moment with your kids count as you present memorable messages, fascinating facts, and awesome Bible enrichment from A to Z!

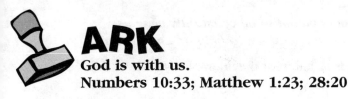

ARK

God is with us.
Numbers 10:33; Matthew 1:23; 28:20

A TO Z SUPPLIES: You'll need a Bible, a decorated box with lid, small containers with lids for kids to decorate, paper and markers, glue, and a variety of craft materials such as sequins, feathers, buttons, ribbon, and glitter.

Before class, place the Bible in the decorated box and close the lid.

SPELLING IT OUT

Hold up the box containing the Bible and say: **I have a special box with something very important inside. Later I'll give you a few clues to see if you can figure out what is in the box. But first, let's discover what the letter A stands for! A is for "ark of the covenant," which was a special box that God's people carried with them into battle.**

This ark was different from Noah's ark. The ark of the covenant wasn't a boat but was a gold-covered box that contained God's promise to his people—kind of a contract between God and Israel. God promised to be with his people, to lead and love them, to help and heal them. And in return, the people promised to love and obey God. When the people had the ark of the covenant before them, they knew God was with them in battle, during worship, or *anytime!* Ask:

- ■ **How did it help the people to know that God was with them all the time?**
- ■ **Why did God want his people to know that he was with them?**
- ■ **Do we need a box today to know that God is with us? Explain.**

Say: **The ark of the covenant disappeared before Jesus was born, and no one knows where it went. But we don't need that box any longer because Jesus is here with us! In fact, one of Jesus' names, Immanuel, means "God is with us!"**

Now let's see if you can guess what's in my special box. Here are the clues!

This item is meant to be constantly near us;
To love us and lead us, to help us and heal us!

Invite kids to tell what they think is in the box, then reveal the Bible inside.

READING THE WORD

Read aloud Numbers 10:33 and Matthew 1:23; 28:20b, then say: **God has promised to stay near us. In Old Testament times, God's promise was kept in the ark of the covenant. But today, we have God's promise of love in Jesus, who is always with us! And we also have the Bible, which is God's Word to help us stay close to God.** Ask:

■ **In what ways is Jesus God's promise to us?**

■ **In what ways does God's Word stay near us?**

■ **How does it help to know that God is always with us?**

Say: **Let's make our own special boxes with God's Word inside to remind us that God is with us all the time!**

Let kids use craft materials to decorate their containers. Have kids write "Surely I am with you always, to the very end of the age" (Matthew 28:20b) on slips of paper to place in their containers. Challenge kids to read the verse every day for the next two weeks.

For he has put everything under his feet

BRICKS

Jesus is our strong foundation.
Exodus 5:6-8; 1 Corinthians 3:10, 11

A TO Z SUPPLIES: You'll need a Bible, a brick, a bucket, water, dirt, dried grass or straw, and aluminum foil.

Kids love to make mud bricks, but this activity is best done out-doors. Have premoistened towelettes handy for quick cleanup. If you want a bit less mess, use self-hardening clay and let kids knead dried grass into the clay before forming their small mud bricks.

SPELLING IT OUT

Set out the brick, the dirt, and the dried grass or straw. Invite kids to look over your "building materials," then ask them to identify the material that would make the sturdiest building and tell why they chose that material. After several kids share their ideas, say: **There are lots of materials to build with, but when you want to build something strong and sturdy, bricks are a good choice. That's why our object talk today, which is based on the letter B, is all about bricks. We'll discover how bricks in Old Testament days were made and what they were used to build. We'll also learn about the strongest cornerstone on which to build our lives!**

Hold up the brick and say: **In Old Testament times, mud bricks were used to build temples, houses, wells, and walls. But the people didn't get their bricks from the building supply center—they had to make them. It was hot, hard work in the blazing sun! You may remember how Pharaoh made the Hebrew slaves make bricks.** Read aloud Exodus 5:6-8. **That was a lot of hard work for God's people!**

Here is how bricks were made in Old Testament times. First, a deep hole was dug in the ground, then it was filled with water. Next, dirt, straw, dried palm-leaf fibers, and bits of shell or pebbles were tossed in the hole. Workers would use their hands or feet to mix the mud into clay, which was formed into blocks or bricks. Finally, the bricks were dried in the sun. Bricks used for the foundations of buildings were dried in kilns or ovens, which made the bricks even stronger! Ask:

- **Why is it important to have a strong foundation on which to build houses?**
- **How do building materials affect how strong the building is?**
- **In what ways is Jesus the perfect choice on which we build our lives?**

READING THE WORD

Read aloud 1 Corinthians 3:10, 11 and 1 Peter 2:6. Say: **Strong bricks were very important in Old Testament times because they made strong foundations for many buildings. Bricks remind us of strong foundations and of how Jesus is the strong foundation on which we build our lives! Let's make some mud bricks as we learn more about laying a strong foundation in our lives.**

Let kids form small groups. Have each group mix dirt, straw or dried grass, and water into thick mud with a clay-like texture, then form the mud into small bricks, one per person. (Use self-hardening clay and dried grass for "cleaner" brick making!) Set the bricks on pieces of aluminum foil to dry in the sun.

When everyone has made a brick, read aloud 1 Corinthians 3:11 again, then ask:

- ■ **How does Jesus' love, forgiveness, and power make our faith strong?**
- ■ **In what ways is a strong building like strong faith?**
- ■ **How does strong faith keep us from falling apart in times of trouble?**

Say: **Bricks were wonderful building materials and strong foundations in Old Testament times, but we have Jesus' power to form our solid foundations! Each time you see bricks this week, say "Jesus is our firm foundation!" Let's thank Jesus for being the strong foundation of our lives.** Pray: **Dear Lord, thank you for giving us a strong foundation of love, forgiveness, and faith on which to build our lives! Amen.** Have kids take their bricks home to use as paperweights or bookends.

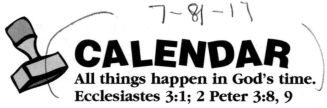

7-81-17

CALENDAR
All things happen in God's time.
Ecclesiastes 3:1; 2 Peter 3:8, 9

A TO Z SUPPLIES: You'll need a Bible, a calendar, self-hardening clay, wax paper or foil, and party toothpicks.

Before class, purchase party toothpicks that are colored and have fluffy cellophane tops on them. These fancy toothpicks are available at any party supply shop and in most party departments at discount stores. Be sure you have two toothpicks for each child.

SPELLING IT OUT

Gather kids and ask them to tell the date. Then hold up a calendar and invite kids to tell important dates we celebrate throughout the year, such as Christmas, birthdays, Easter, and Valentine's Day. Then lead kids in the old Mother Goose rhyme telling the number of days in each month:

Thirty days bath September,
April, June, and November;

February has twenty-eight alone,
All the rest have thirty-one,
Excepting leap year, that's the time
When February's days are twenty-nine.

Say: **Calendars help us mark days, months, and special times throughout the year. Keeping track of time and celebrations was also important during Old Testament times. The letter C is for calendar, so today we'll discover what Old Testament calendars were like and how, although we assign special dates to events, all things happen in God's time!**
The first calendars we know about from Old Testament times were from the days when God's people in Canaan were under Egyptian rule. The days began at sunrise and ended when the sun set; nighttime was the time in between. There was a twelve month calendar just as we have, but each of their months only had thirty days, so they had five extra days at the end of the year. The thirty days of each month were marked by placing wooden pegs into holes on a clay slab, so when all the holes were filled, the people knew that a new month was beginning. But even though God's people knew there were many special days to mark and remember, they knew that all things happen in God's time! Ask:

■ **Why is it good that God controls time and people do not?**
■ **How does it help our faith to know that all things happen in God's time?**
■ **How can knowing this help us be more patient?**

READING THE WORD

Read Jeremiah 5:24b; Ecclesiastes 3:1; and 2 Peter 3:8, 9. Say: **The Bible tells us that all things happen according to God's will and in his time. God is in control of time and events, and our job isn't to rush God—it's to wait on him!** Ask:

■ **How does knowing all things happen in God's time help us when we pray? when ask for God's help?**
■ **What else is God in control of besides time?**
■ **In what ways does God's control of everything show us his love?**

Say: **Let's make cool Canaan calendars to remind us that all things happen in God's time. We can use our calendars**

N
O
P
Q
R
S
T
U
V
W
X
Y
Z

9

Remote control car
Isaiah 14:27
Psalm 37:23
Hebrews 2:8
James 4:7
Proverbs 19-21
Romans 12-?

to mark times we pray and thank God for being in control of time, events, and the whole world!

Have each child flatten a piece of self-hardening clay into a ½-inch-thick rectangle about 6-by-3-inches in size. Let kids use the fancy toothpicks to poke holes in the clay tablets. Make four rows of seven holes and a fifth row with three holes for a total of thirty-one holes, which represent the days of the month. (Be sure kids remove the toothpicks so the clay around the holes can harden.) After the clay has hardened, kids can use a toothpick to mark the days of the month. Move the toothpick each day and be sure to offer thank-yous to God for his power and control in the world.

DONKEY

It's important to listen to God!
Numbers 22:21-31; Luke 11:28; John 8:47

A TO Z SUPPLIES: You'll need a Bible, an enlarged copy of the donkey from the margin, tape, markers, and brown construction paper.

Before class, either photocopy or draw an enlarged version of the donkey in the margin. Color the donkey and cut it out. Tape the donkey to a wall, the door, or a chalkboard at children's arm level. Tear a pair of brown paper donkey ears for each child.

SPELLING IT OUT

Hand each child a pair of paper donkey ears. Say: **These paper ears remind us of a type of animal that we read about in the Bible. The animal begins with the letter D and has very big ears. Which animal do you think our Old Testament object talk is about today?** After kids share their guesses, say: **Donkeys have large ears, and *donkey* begins with the letter D. Let's see if you can "pin" the ears on this donkey!** Take turns having kids close their eyes and trying to tape the ears on the donkey.

When everyone has had a turn, say: **Did you know there was a talking donkey in the Old Testament? That's right, a donkey listened to God, then spoke to his owner. Today we'll discover how that stubborn donkey teaches us us about the importance of listening to God.**

Long ago lived a man named Balaam who had a faithful donkey. Balaam didn't listen to God very carefully and didn't always obey him either. Once Balaam took his donkey and left to put a curse on God's people. God knew Balaam didn't listen well, so he sent an angel to appear in the path before the donkey. Balaam's donkey stopped. No matter how many times Balaam beat the donkey, it wouldn't budge! That's because the donkey had seen an angel and was listening to God. Balaam didn't listen to God, but when the donkey spoke, Balaam listened! The donkey told Balaam that there was an angel in the road, and suddenly Balaam saw—and listened! Ask:

- **In what way did the donkey listen to God?**
- **Why was it good that the donkey listened to God through the angel?**
- **Why is it important for us to listen to God?**

Say: **Balaam's donkey did what Balaam didn't do—he listened to God and obeyed him. Let's see what the Bible says about listening to God.**

READING THE WORD

Read aloud Numbers 22:21-31; Luke 11:28; and John 8:47, then ask:

- **What did Balaam learn about listening to God?**
- **In what ways can we listen to God?**
- **How are listening to God and obeying him related?**

Say: **Balaam's donkey listened to God and spoke words of wisdom, too. It's important to listen to God's Word not only through our ears, but also through our hearts and actions. Let's write God's wise words on the paper donkey ears to remind us of the importance of listening to God.**

Have kids write "He who belongs to God" (from John 8:47) on one of the donkey ears and "hears what God says" on the other ear. Challenge kids to be stubborn in learning God's Word this week by learning the verse on the donkey ears. End with a prayer thanking God for giving us ears to hear and hearts to obey him.

ELIJAH
God is in control.
1 Kings 17:6; Jeremiah 10:12, 13

A TO Z SUPPLIES: You'll need a Bible, photocopies of the poem strip from page 13, and black craft feathers.

Before class, be sure you have a black craft feather for each child. These can be purchased at most craft stores.

SPELLING IT OUT

Gather kids in a circle and stand in the center holding a black feather. Tell kids you're going to toss the feather in the air and have them stand at the place in the room where they think the feather will land. Repeat this activity several times, then say: **It's kind of a guessing game to predict where the feather will land, isn't it? That's because we're not in control of the feather or in control of how other things happen in the world. Today we'll learn how God's prophet Elijah was helped by a feathery bird that God controlled. E is for Elijah, who knew that only God is in control of everything!**

Hand each child a black craft feather and say: **Each time you hear the word** *control,* **flap your feathers like a bird. God chose a man named Elijah to be his prophet. Elijah knew that God was in** *control* **and would tell him what to say to the people. Through his prophet Elijah, God** *controlled* **when it rained and when it would stop raining. And God told Elijah the words to say to his people. Once Elijah obeyed God by hiding near a stream. Elijah was hungry, but he knew God was in** *control!* **God sent a black-as-night raven to bring Elijah scraps of food. God** *controlled* **the raven to help Elijah, and I'm sure Elijah was happy that God was in** *control!* Read aloud 1 Kings 17:6, then ask:

■ **In what ways did God's control help Elijah?**
■ **How does God's control help us today?**

READING THE WORD

Ask a volunteer to read aloud Jeremiah 10:12, 13 and Psalm 91:11. Then say: **Because God made the world, he controls all things in it. Through God's wisdom and power, all things are under his command—even us. So we can rely** on God to keep things under his control when we're worried or mad, hopeful or sad. Ask:

- ■ **What is God in control of?**
- ■ **How does it help our faith to know God is in control?**

Say: **So many things in our lives seem "up in the air"** (toss the feather in the air), **and we often wonder and worry about how they will turn out. It's important to remember that God is in control and that all things are in his powerful hands! So let's make floating feathers to remind us that even though we don't control things, God does!**

Distribute copies of the poem strip and read it aloud. Then have kids poke the ends of their feathers down and up through one end of the poem almost like a sewing stitch.

End by forming a circle and offering a prayer thanking God for his perfect control over all the world and our lives. After saying "amen," have everyone toss a feather in the air and say, "God is in control!"

> *Remember what Elijah knew*
> *when a feather falls from your hand—*
> *That God is in complete control*
> *of where everything will land!*

FOOTWEAR
We can follow where God leads.
Deuteronomy 27:10; Ephesians 6:7

A TO Z SUPPLIES: You'll need a Bible, a pair of sandals, scissors, a stapler, an old file folder and pencil, and sheets of thin foam rubber (available at most craft stores).

Before class, purchase two squares of thin foam rubber for each child. This is colorful, flexible foam about ⅛-inch thick. (If you can't find the foam rubber, substitute colorful poster board. Kids will be making sandals, and you'll need one large sheet of poster board for every two kids.) Use the file folder to make a pattern for the sandals by enlarging the drawing in the margin of page 14 to about 8 inches long or the size as most of your kids' feet.

SPELLING IT OUT

Hold up the pair of sandals and ask kids to identify this type of footwear. Then invite kids to compare and contrast sandals with tennis shoes or dress shoes they might wear today. Say: **Sandals are different from regular shoes, aren't they? People have been wearing sandals since they started wearing shoes. Though some of the poorest people in Old Testament times went barefoot, most wore sandals as footwear. Footwear begins with the letter F and is the subject of our object talk today. We'll be discovering what footwear God's people wore and how footwear helped people walk great distances to follow God.**

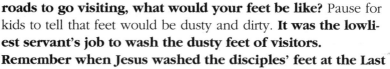

The Hebrews wore leather sandals that went between their first two toes and were tied around their ankles with leather laces. Their footwear was always removed before going into someone's house as a sign of respect. But just think: if you walked a great way over dusty roads to go visiting, what would your feet be like? Pause for kids to tell that feet would be dusty and dirty. **It was the lowliest servant's job to wash the dusty feet of visitors. Remember when Jesus washed the disciples' feet at the Last Supper? This was to show them that he had come as a servant to all people and that we can serve others, too. This is what God desires, and it is a good way to follow God!**

People served God by walking long distances, too. Abraham followed God's calling to Canaan and walked all the way in his sandals. And when God called Moses to lead his people away from Pharaoh, sandals helped carry him along.

■ **Why is following God important?**
■ **What ways can we follow God with our feet? hands? hearts?**

READING THE WORD

Ask a volunteer to read aloud Deuteronomy 27:10; Joshua 24:14a; and Ephesians 6:7. Then say: **Wearing sandals helped God's people go to great lengths to serve and follow him.**

From soldiers marching in God's campaigns to prophets going to other lands to carry God's words, footwear played an important role in following God. But of course, it takes more than sandals or feet to follow God, doesn't it? **What does it take to be a good follower of God?** Lead kids to realize that a willing heart, great faith, and trusting God are all vital to following him.

Say: **Let's make super sandals to wear as reminders that we need always to be ready, willing, and able to follow and serve God.**

Have kids use the sandal pattern to trace and cut out pairs of sandals. Cut along the dotted line, then fold the flap forward and staple it on the short line. Slide the sandals on between the first and second toes. Wear your sandals as you thank God for the ability and willingness to follow him at all times.

GRAIN
God provides for us.
Psalms 65:9; 111:4, 5; John 6:35

A TO Z SUPPLIES: You'll need a Bible, a loaf of whole-grain bread, honey, plastic knives, shelled sunflower seeds, and napkins.

Before class, make sure your whole-grain bread is sliced into enough slices for each child to have at least half a slice. If you can find small bags of toasted barley or wheat, this is a nice extra touch for discovering how different grains taste! Check out your local natural food store for a great variety of grains to sprinkle on your bread.

SPELLING IT OUT

Set out the loaf of bread and ask kids to explain how this bread might have been made. Cut a small slice for each child to taste, then have kids save the rest of their bread for later. Say: **Bread is made from grains such as wheat, barley, corn, and more. Grain was very important in biblical days, and**

the people looked to God to provide good growing conditions for their crops. Today we'll discover why grain was a staple food for the Hebrews and how God provided the grain and other foods his people needed to live.

In Old Testament times, October through April was a time for plowing and planting seeds. Everyone in the family helped sow the seeds and weed the fields. They would scatter seeds from a basket as they walked up and down the length of the field. Farmers planted wheat, barley, rye, and millet. In the months of May through September, all the grain was harvested. Ask:

- How did God help during the growing season?
- How is tending a field like taking care of the way our faith grows?

Explain that growing faith means "weeding" out negative thoughts and "watering" generously with love for God! Then continue: Each day, every day, the women and children would grind the grain for that day's fresh bread. God provided the grain and the conditions to grow it. Faithful farmers tended the fields, and hard-working women made the grain into nutritious bread. Everyone was thankful for God's provision of grain, and they had great feasts to celebrate.

READING THE WORD

Invite volunteers to read aloud Psalms 65:9; 111:4, 5; and John 6:35. Ask:

- In what ways was bread vital to life in Old Testament times?
- How is Jesus vital to our lives today, just as bread is?
- How does God provide for us through grain and other good foods? through his Son Jesus?

Say: God provides for every need we have. He feeds us with good foods and nourishes us with Jesus' love. God's provision of grains keeps us healthy during our lifetimes, and his loving provision of Jesus keeps us alive now and eternally when we accept Jesus as our Savior! Now that's what I call perfect provision!

Let kids spread honey on slices of bread, then sprinkle on sunflower seeds and other grains you desire. Before eating your treats, share a prayer thanking God for providing good grains and foods as well as Jesus in our lives.

HEBREW

We are God's people!
Deuteronomy 14:2; John 1:12, 13; 1 Peter 2:9

A TO Z SUPPLIES: You'll need a Bible, a family tree of your own or from a book, sandpaper, scissors, tape, newsprint or poster board, markers, and green construction paper.

Before class, draw a large family tree like the one on page 18 on a large piece of newsprint or poster board. Tape the family tree to the wall.

SPELLING IT OUT

Hold up a family tree from a book or your own family tree if you have one. Gather kids in front of the family tree. Ask kids to identify what this "tree" is and what family trees are used for. Then say: **Family trees help us learn about the people in our families and who lived before us. We can learn a lot about our own lives by looking at our ancestors. God's people in the Old Testament were first called Hebrews, which starts with the letter H. Today we'll learn the different names for the people in God's family tree and how we're all part of the family of God.**

Point to the chart on the wall. Say: **The Hebrews are mentioned many times in the Old Testament—they are the family of people who knew, loved, and followed God. Daniel was a Hebrew who kept praying to God even when a king told him not to. David was a Hebrew who grew up to be king after he had killed the giant Goliath. And Jacob was a Hebrew who tricked his brother into their father's inheritance.**

When God called Jacob, he promised to make Jacob and his relatives into a strong nation. After God changed Jacob's name to *Israel,* God's people were not only called Hebrews but also *Israelites.* In other words, Israelites were Hebrews! Later, the Israelites divided into twelve tribes. Let's read their names.

Ask volunteers to read aloud the twelve tribes of Israel from the family-tree chart, then say: **After many years the tribe of Judah came to be called *Jews,* and from the tribe of Judah a very special member of God's family was born! Who do**

N
O
P
Q
R
S
T
U
V
W
X
Y
Z

you think that was? **It was Jesus! Jesus was a Hebrew, an Israelite, a Jew, and, most importantly, God's Son!** Ask:

- **Is the name of our nationality or family important to God? Explain.**
- **How are we all related to God and part of his family?**

READING THE WORD

Say: **All these names can be confusing when we read them in the Bible, but they all describe God's family.** Read aloud Deuteronomy 14:2; John 1:12, 13; and 1 Peter 2:9. Then say: **Did the family tree stop after Jesus was born? Nope—it just got bigger! Jesus came for all who believe in him and accept him as their Savior and Lord. After the Jews, the Gentiles accepted Jesus, and soon we all became one in God's family of believers! That's a pretty wonderful family to be a part of, isn't it? Let's make family-tree bookmarks to remind us that we're all part of God's family when we know, love, and accept his Son Jesus.**

Have kids cut sandpaper tree trunks, then each tear six green paper leaves and tape them to the trees. On the lowest leaves write the words "Hebrew" and "Israelite." On the next two leaves, write "Jew" and "Gentile." And on the top two leaves, write "Jesus" and "Me!" Have kids write their own names on the Me leaves. End with a prayer thanking God for the gift of being part of his special family.

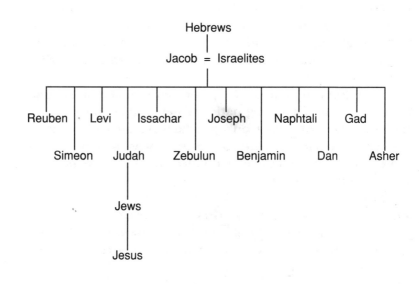

Hebrews | Jacob = Israelites

Reuben | Levi | Issachar | Joseph | Naphtali | Gad
Simeon | Judah | Zebulun | Benjamin | Dan | Asher

Jews

Jesus

INHERITANCE

God gives us his blessings.
Leviticus 20:24; Ephesians 1:18, 19

A TO Z SUPPLIES: You'll need a Bible, a large candy bar, a plastic knife, satin cord, and a number of keys.

Before class, be sure you have a key for each child. Blank keys can generally be purchased anywhere keys are made, such as hardware stores. Make sure the keys have holes at one end to slide satin cord through to make necklaces. Cut a 16-inch length of satin cord for each child.

SPELLING IT OUT

Gather kids and have them figure out who is the oldest in the class, then who is the oldest boy in the room. Hand the oldest boy the large candy bar. Be prepared for indignant shouts of "No fair!" (This is exactly what you want!) Say: **Well, I can see that some of you feel slighted! But this is exactly what used to happen every day in Old Testament times. The oldest boy in a family would receive what is called an inheritance from his father. A father would give his land, flocks, and treasures to his oldest son as his inheritance. The word *inheritance* begins with the letter I, and today we'll learn about inheritances and why we all have an inheritance in God's kingdom today.** (Make sure the child with the candy doesn't eat it yet—you'll divide it up later.)

Yes, the oldest son was usually the one who would receive his father's inheritance. Sometimes a younger son would have a portion of the inheritance, but a girl could only inherit if there were no brothers in the family. Remember the story of how Jacob tricked his brother Esau out of his inheritance? In Old Testament times inheritances were very important because they carried on the wealth or the work the father had begun. And inheritances passed down through generations, but as you can see, an inheritance was not meant for everyone. Ask:

■ **How did it feel not to receive a candy bar?**
■ **Why did it feel unfair?**

Say: **Now let's see how God passed a wonderful inheritance on to us!**

READING THE WORD

Ask volunteers to read aloud Leviticus 20:24; 1 Peter 1:3, 4; and Ephesians 1:18, 19. Then say: **The greatest treasure and inheritance God has given us is his Son, Jesus! And God didn't just send Jesus for the oldest in our families or just for the males. God gives his Son to all of us when we love and accept Jesus into our lives. When we know, love, and follow Jesus, we have a special inheritance in the kingdom of heaven. In other words, we share in the greatest inheritance of all!** Divide up the candy bar so each person has a small taste.

Continue: **God has given us the keys** (hold up a key) **to the kingdom of heaven through his Son, Jesus Christ! Isn't that awesome? Let's make inheritance keys to remind us that we have a heavenly inheritance in God's kingdom!**

Let each child choose a key, then demonstrate how to loop the satin cord through the holes in the keys. Push a loop through the hole in the key, then thread the two ends of the cord through the loop and pull it tight. Tie the ends of the cord to make necklaces. When everyone is wearing a key, share a prayer thanking God for your inheritance in God's kingdom through Jesus Christ.

JONAH
God forgives us.
Daniel 9:9; Jonah 2:9, 10; Ephesians 4:32

A TO Z SUPPLIES: You'll need a Bible, a medium-sized box, white poster board, clear balloons, permanent markers, and jelly beans.

Before class, find a box large enough for kids to crawl through. Then turn the box into a giant fish by cutting off the end flaps to make a "tunnel." Decorate the fish with paper fins, then cut out two sets of large teeth and tape them to one end of the box for an open mouth. Be sure you have a balloon and a jelly bean for each child.

SPELLING IT OUT

Set the box fish to one side of the room and gather kids on the opposite side. Invite kids to tell about times they were given another chance to do what was right after they had done something wrong, such as telling a lie. Then ask kids why second chances are good and helpful. Say: **Do you remember the story of Jonah and how he was swallowed by the giant fish? Jonah begins with the letter J, and today we'll learn how God gave Jonah a second chance. We'll also discover that God is the God of second chances because he forgives us.**

God told Jonah to go and warn the people of Nineveh that they were being disobedient, but Jonah didn't like those people and was afraid they would hurt him. What did Jonah do? He ran and hid in a boat. But can we hide from God? No way! When the sea grew stormy, Jonah knew he was at fault and he jumped overboard to save the sailors from sinking. Did Jonah die in the water? No way! God gave him a second chance! God sent a big fish to swallow Jonah.

Have kids "swim" to the box fish and crawl through the mouth. Continue: **Jonah knew he had disobeyed God and was sorry for disobeying. For three days Jonah prayed inside the fish and asked for God's forgiveness. Did God keep him inside the fish? No way! God forgave Jonah and had the fish spit him out on the land.** Have kids crawl out of the fish through its mouth.

Say: **God had forgiven Jonah and given him another chance to obey. And Jonah ran straight to the town to warn the people!**

READING THE WORD

Ask volunteers to read aloud Jonah 2:9, 10; Daniel 9:9; and Ephesians 4:32. Then ask:
- **In what ways did God give Jonah second chances?**
- **How does God give us second chances?**
- **How do we know that Jonah was forgiven?**
- **How are God's forgiveness and second chances demonstrations of his great love?**

Say: **God forgives us when we admit our wrongs and sincerely ask for his forgiveness. And God doesn't hold grudges! God is the God of second chances. God gives us another chance to do the right thing because he loves us and wants us to do right more than he wants to punish us. Think silently about something you might need to ask God's forgiveness for. Later we'll say a quiet prayer asking God's**

forgiveness, but right now let's make Jonah balloons to remind us that God forgives us and gives us another chance!

Hand each child a balloon and a jelly bean. Have kids gently push their jelly-bean "Jonahs" through the balloon openings. Inflate the balloons and tie the ends. Have kids use markers to decorate the balloons to look like fish.

End by praying: **Dear God, I want to ask your forgiveness for** (have kids silently think of the thing for which they need forgiveness). **We thank you for your loving forgiveness and for giving us second chances to do the right thing! Amen.**

KING DAVID
God sees us on the inside!
1 Samuel 16:7; Romans 12:12-18

A TO Z SUPPLIES: You'll need a Bible, scissors, poster board, clear packing tape, tacky craft glue, markers, sequins, and plastic jewels.

Before class, be sure you have a variety of plastic jewels and sequins. Kids will be making cool crowns and will attach "gems-n-jewels" to their crowns. You'll also need to make a crown or wear a "diamond" headband or tiara for this object talk.

SPELLING IT OUT

Wear your crown and say: **I'm wearing a symbol of some-one who was looked on as the "big cheese" of a country or land long ago. This person had an important job of leading the people in his land. Some of the people who wore this headpiece were good and kind, but some were mean and cruel! Who wore this type of headpiece?** Let kids tell that it's a king's or queen's crown. Then ask:

■ **In what ways could a king hurt or help his people?**
■ **What kind of king would God approve of? Explain.**

Say: **K is for "king," and today we'll learn about King David and why he was God's choice to lead God's people. We'll also discover how God looked at King David—and how he looks at each of us today!**

King David wasn't always a king. When he was young, he was a simple shepherd boy who had seven older brothers. Young David was brave and had even killed bears and lions to protect the sheep in his flock. David loved to play the hand harp and sing poems to God. That's because David's heart was full of love for God! Ask the following questions. Before a child answers, let her put on the crown.

- ■ **What qualities did David have to be king?**
- ■ **How did David's love for God make him brave?**

Continue: **When David was still a boy, God sent Samuel to set David aside as chosen by God to be the next king of Israel. Wow! Imagine David's surprise when he was so young and small! But remember, David's love for God was huge! That's why David was able to kill the mean giant Goliath! What did people see when they looked at David? They saw a young lad who wasn't very big or special-looking. But what did God see? Let's find out!**

READING THE WORD

Read aloud 1 Samuel 16:7. Then ask the following questions, letting the children who answer wear the crown.

- ■ **What did God see when he looked at David?**
- ■ **How does looking at our hearts tell who we really are inside?**
- ■ **What do you think was in David's heart?**

Say: **David had immense love and bravery in his heart. He was honest and true; he was loving and protective. In other words, David was a "man after God's own heart." That tells us a lot about what God is like, doesn't it? Later, as King David, he was a king after God's own heart. How can we be people after God's own heart? The Bible gives us clues!**

Read aloud Romans 12:12-18, then say: **God wants us to be people of honesty, love, kindness, and faith. And remember, this is what God looks for when he looks inside our hearts! Now let's make crowns to remind us that we're all King's kids when we have hearts of love for God.**

Let kids create cool crowns from wide strips of poster board. Measure the strips to fit around kids' heads, then use clear packing tape to secure the ends. Decorate the crowns by gluing on sequins and plastic jewels. Write on the crowns, "God sees inside our hearts!"

LAMB

We follow the Good Shepherd.
Psalm 23:1, 2; John 10:11

A TO Z SUPPLIES: You'll need a Bible, fiber fill, craft glue, scissors, poster board, tape, brass paper fasteners, craft sticks, markers, and the lamb pattern from page 25.

Before class, enlarge and cut out several poster-board patterns of the lamb pattern on page 25. Be sure you have two craft sticks and two brass paper fasteners for each child.

SPELLING IT OUT

Gather kids and say: I have a riddle for you. Let's see if you can guess which animal I'm talking about.

> *I play Follow the Leader wherever I go;*
> *I always wear fleece that's as white as the snow.*
> *Who am I?*

Ask kids to tell you their ideas, then hold up a clump of fiber fill and say: **Yes, the clues were for a lamb or sheep. Here is a bit of fluff that feels much like lamb's wool.** Pass the "fleece" around the room as you say: **Sheep are mentioned often in the Bible, especially in the Old Testament. Today we'll discover some interesting facts about sheep and how we're a bit like sheep, too! Then we'll make neat Follow-the-Leader Lambs as we learn more about following Jesus.**

Many men and boys in the Old Testament were shepherds and took care of flocks of sheep. They protected their lambs, fed them, and led them to cool water and green pastures. Once a year, shepherds sheared their sheep to make robes and tents. Sheep were important to shepherds—and shepherds were important to sheep, too! The sheep knew their shepherd's voice and followed him everywhere with great trust. Ask:

- **How are sheep following shepherds with trust similar to the way we follow Jesus with trust?**
- **Why did shepherds care about their sheep so greatly? How does Jesus care for us?**

READING THE WORD

Read aloud Psalm 23:1, 2 and John 10:11, then say: **Jesus tells us that he is our Good Shepherd and that we are his flock. We can trust Jesus to keep us safe and provide for our needs. And as good lambs in Jesus' flock, we know his voice and want nothing more than to follow him with love and faith!** Ask:

- **In what ways is Jesus our Good Shepherd?**
- **How does it help us to know, love, and follow Jesus?**
- **In what ways can we follow Jesus?**

Show kids how to trace and cut out the lamb and the lamb's legs from poster board. Attach the legs to the lambs' bodies using paper fasteners, then tape the lambs' feet to craft sticks. Finally, use markers to add faces and ears, then glue bits of fiber fill to the lambs. When you're finished, show kids how to make the lambs kick up their heels for joy by moving the craft sticks up and down.

Use your lively lambs to play a quick game of Follow the Leader. If there's time, write "I am the good shepherd" (John 10:11) on the backs of the lambs.

METHUSELAH
God is the same yesterday and today.
Genesis 5:25-27; Psalm 119:89-91

A TO Z SUPPLIES: You'll need a Bible, tube icing, cupcakes, and a birthday candle for each child.

No prior preparation required.

SPELLING IT OUT

Hand each child a birthday candle and explain that you're going to play a game. Say: **In this crazy game, I'll call out a** number. You must work together to form a group or groups with that many candles. If there are kids left over, they'll be the candle-counters. Be sure to hold your candles high so we can count them!

Call out low numbers such as four, seven, five, and one. End by calling out 969 and wait for everyone to giggle, gasp, or shout, "You can't do that!" Then say: **I guess 969 *would* be a lot of candles on a birthday cake, wouldn't it? But today we'll learn about a man in the Old Testament who really was that old! And we'll also discover that God is eternal and never changes—no matter how many years go by!** Invite kids to sit in place and hold their candles.

Read aloud Genesis 5:25-27, then say: **Methuselah certainly had a lot of birthdays, didn't he! Imagine if we had lived 969 years ago; it would barely have been the year 1000! Methuselah was very old and the father of many children. In fact, he was Noah's grandpa. And at 969 years old, just think of all the birthdays Methuselah celebrated! Is there anyone who hasn't had a birthday at all?**

Allow time for kids to respond, then say: **There *is* someone we know and love who has never had a regular birthday— that someone is God! God is eternal and always was and always will be. And even through all of our birthdays, God doesn't change. We can trust God today to be just as loving and faithful as he was yesterday and will be tomorrow!**

READING THE WORD

Read aloud Psalm 119:89-91 and Jeremiah 10:10. Then ask:
- **What things remain the same with God?** (Answers might include God's love, forgiveness, and power.)
- **Why is it good that God never changes?**
- **How does it help our faith to know that God is eternal and unchanging?**

Say: **God is the same today as he was yesterday and will be tomorrow! When we read in the Old Testament about God's faithfulness to Methuselah or Noah, we can count on God to be just as faithful to us today. Isn't that wonderful? Let's have a celebration for God and tell him how glad we are that he is eternal and always the same.**

Let kids use the tube icing to decorate cupcakes, then place their candles in the treats. Form a circle and say: **Methuselah had 969 birthdays to celebrate. But God doesn't need a** birthday because he is eternal, which means he always was and always will be with us. It was God who created people and birthdays. Isn't it wonderful to know that our God is a forever God who will always remain faithful, loving, and all-powerful? Let's offer God a prayer of thanks for his eternal presence. Hold your cakes and candles in front of you. Pray: **Dear God, we thank you for birthdays and celebrations of life. But most of all, we thank you for being eternal and for never changing. We love you! Amen.**

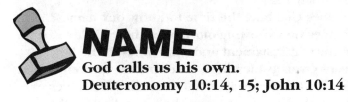

NAME
God calls us his own.
Deuteronomy 10:14, 15; John 10:14

A TO Z SUPPLIES: You'll need a Bible, a book of baby names, pencils, markers, tape, construction paper, and bulletin-board letters.

Before class, punch out the bulletin-board letters if needed. Kids will be tracing letters to make their names. For younger kids or for small groups, you may wish to purchase several sets of pre-cut letters. Kids will need enough letters to make their names twice.

SPELLING IT OUT

Have kids form a circle and take turns using the baby name book to look up meaning for their names. If someone's name is not in the book, have others suggest a meaning for that person's name, such as "nice smile" or "someone who is kind."

Say: **Names are important, aren't they? We name people because certain names sound pretty or were in the family already. Back in Old Testament times, names were given to people because of their meanings. I'll tell you a meaning, and you see if you can figure out whose name it was.** Read the following meanings (the names are in parentheses).

- ■ *God is with us* (Immanuel)
- ■ *the man* (Adam)
- ■ *father of many* (Abraham)
- ■ *he laughs* (Isaac)
- ■ *the rock* (Peter)
- ■ *the Lord saves* (Jesus)

A
B
C
D
E
F
G
H
I
J
K
L
M

Say: **It's fun to learn what different names mean. Did you know that God had Adam give all the animals their names? That's because God wanted us all to have names— even the animals.** Ask:

- **Why are names a part of who we are?**
- **Does anyone know all the names in the world? Explain.**

READING THE WORD

Invite volunteers to read aloud Deuteronomy 10:14, 15 and John 10:14. Then ask:

- **Why does God take the time to know our names?**
- **How does God knowing our names show his love for us?**

Say: **In the Old Testament and sometimes in the New, names were given as blessings, descriptions, or even hopes. Sometimes God told parents what to name their babies or changed people's names to show their new lives in the Lord. For example, God changed Abram's name to Abraham in the Old Testament, and Saul's name was changed to Paul in the New Testament. But of all the names God knows, we all have the same name in God's family. When we love and follow God, he calls us _his!_ Let's make cool name plaques and write the meanings of our names on them.**

Have kids trace on construction paper and cut out two of each letter in their names. Tape individual letters together to make two names, then tape one upside down on top of the other to make a "mirror image." Invite kids to use markers to write a meaning for their names that shows how they feel or think concerning God. Suggestions might include "prays to God" or "keeps the Lord first." Have kids hang their mirror plaques on their mirrors at home and each time they see them, repeat, "I am called God's child." End by sharing your new name meanings and a prayer thanking God for calling us his.

OLIVE OIL
God chooses us to serve him.
1 Samuel 16:12, 13; Colossians 3:12

A TO Z SUPPLIES: You'll need a Bible, a small jar of green olives, a small bottle of olive oil, colored vinyl tape, satin cord, scissors, cotton balls, and small plastic vials (available from pharmacies or doctors' offices).

Before class, be sure you have a small plastic vial for each child. These vials are the type that hold medication and are usually clear or a brown tint. Be sure the vials have snap-on tops. Cut a 16-inch length of satin cord for each child.

SPELLING IT OUT

Hold up the jar of olives and ask kids to identify this food, then give each child an olive to taste. Invite kids to name foods that they like to eat with olives. Suggestions might include pizza, potato-chip dips, or salads. Say: **Olives were important to people in Old Testament days. They ate olives at almost every meal and used olive oil in various ways. Here's a bottle of oil that was squeezed from green olives like the kind you just tasted. "Olive" and "oil" both begin with the letter O, and today we'll discover what olive oil was used for and how it was used to bless people who served God. We'll also learn that God chooses whom he will use in his service.**

Let each child have a bit of olive oil to rub on his fingers to feel the oily texture, then taste. Say: **Olive trees grew all over biblical lands. It took fifteen years for an olive tree to produce its fruit, but once it did, it would give olives for hundreds of years more! Olives were picked from September to November. Olives were put in a basket and either trampled on by feet to squeeze out the oil or pressed under a very heavy stone. The greasy oil would run into jugs and vats. Olive oil was used in cooking, to fuel oil lamps, and also as a soothing balm for dry skin. When powdered flowers and herbs were added to olive oil, it made perfume for women to wear on their skin and in their hair.**

Olive oil was also used for anointing. Anointing was when a priest or other special follower of God would place a drop or two of olive oil on someone's head or forehead as a sign the person had been chosen by God for a special mission or blessing! Even in the New Testament we know anointing was done, as when Jesus' feet were anointed by Mary as a sign of her great love and reverence for him. In the Old Testament, Samuel anointed young David before he went to fight the giant Goliath. Samuel anointed David to show that David had been chosen and blessed by God for a special mission. David had been set apart to God as special!

- How do you think David felt being set apart for God?
- How does it feel to know God chooses us to serve him?

READING THE WORD

Read aloud 1 Samuel 16:12, 13 and Colossians 3:12. Then say: **God knows us by the love and faith in our hearts. And God knows who he can use to accomplish his will. In other words, God will use whomever he chooses! When we love and follow God, we can serve him in so many ways!** Ask:
- **In what ways can we serve God?**
- **How are we *all* able to be used by God?**

Say: **Let's make special anointing bottles to remind us how we are God's special people and chosen by God to serve him.**

Have kids use bits of colored tape to decorate their plastic vials. Tape a length of cord to the sides of each vial to make them into necklaces. Pour a bit of olive oil on each cotton ball, and let each child place a cotton ball inside her vial.

End by having kids form pairs or trios and let them daub the olive oil on the backs of each other's hands as they say, "You've been chosen by God to serve him!"

PRAYER

God listens to and answers our prayers.
Psalm 34:17; 1 Thessalonians 5:17

A TO Z SUPPLIES: You'll need a Bible, a shawl or scarf, permanent markers, tacky craft glue, fabric fringe or tassels, and a 18-by-24-inch length of white cotton for each child.

Before class, cut white cotton, muslin, or even a clean white bedsheet into 18-by-24-inch rectangles. Kids will be making prayer shawls with the fabric.

SPELLING IT OUT

Put the shawl or scarf around your shoulders. Then say: **I want to pray, but what's the best way? Should I sit or kneel or stand—what should I do with my head and my hands? How will I know that God is near? What special thing do I say so he will hear?** Pause for a moment, then ask:

A B C D E F G H I J K L M

- What is prayer? Is one way better than another to pray?
- Why is prayer a good way to talk with God?

Say: **There are many places and times to pray; there are many ways and words to use in praying to God. But one thing never changes—God always hears and answers our prayers! Today we'll learn how people prayed in the Old Testament and how God heard and answered their prayers just as he does for us today. Then we'll make cool prayer shawls to remind us to pray every day.**

Prayer began when Adam and Eve first talked to God. We're not told much about how they prayed or what they said to God, but we do know that by the time Noah lived and built the ark, he not only prayed to God but listened for God's answers! Noah is the first person we read about who built an altar to God as a sign of humble thanksgiving and praise.

Moses prayed to God when he needed help in freeing the Hebrews from the mean Egyptian pharaoh—and God heard and answered in an amazing way. God parted the Red Sea so his people could escape slavery! Wow—what an answer to prayer! After Moses, the Hebrews began to make prayer shawls to wear during the times that they worshiped, praised, and prayed to God. They considered the shawls a sign of covering up in respect for God. Shawls remind me of a warm hug, too. Maybe God's people felt loved and hugged when they prayed to God! Ask:

- How does praying to God show him our love?
- In what ways does God hearing and answering our prayers show us his love?

READING THE WORD

Read aloud Psalm 34:17; Proverbs 15:29; and 1 Thessalonians 5:17. Then say: **Isn't it wonderful that God loves us enough to hear and answer every prayer we pray? The Hebrews in Old Testament times also knew that God hears and answers prayers, so they took prayer very seriously. They even wore prayer shawls as they prayed to show that it was a special time between themselves and God. Prayer shawls were often made from dyed sheep's wool that was woven into bright colors. Sometimes tassels or trim were added to the edges. These shawls were only worn during times of prayer and worship.** Ask:

- **Do we need any special clothes or ways to pray? Explain.**
- **Does God always answer prayers the way we want him to? Why or why not?**
- **What do we need to pray and talk to God?**
- **How does it help our faith to know that God hears and answers prayer?**

Lead kids to realize that we need a loving spirit, a sincere heart, and a humble attitude when we pray. It doesn't matter if we're angry or sad or happy or afraid—we must have an honest heart before God. Invite children to use markers and fabric trim glued to the short edges of the shawls to decorate their own prayer shawls. Then let kids wear their special prayer shawls as you share a prayer thanking God for always hearing and answering our prayers in his time and in his way.

QUAIL
God gives us what we need.
Exodus 16:12, 13; 2 Peter 1:3

A TO Z SUPPLIES: You'll need a Bible, a picture of a quail, paper plates, lettuce, cold chicken breasts (¼ cooked chicken breast for each child), raisins, mayonnaise, and plastic forks.

Before class, be sure you have a small portion of cold, cooked and boneless chicken breast for each child. You'll be making cool quail salads to nibble later in the object talk. Check in animal books or an encyclopedia for a picture of a quail. If you can bring in a recording of a quail call, that would be extra fun!

SPELLING IT OUT

Place the paper plates, lettuce leaves, plastic forks, raisins, and mayonnaise on a table. Set aside the cold chicken breasts.

Hold up the picture of the quail and ask kids if they can identify this funny little bird. Give the following clues to help kids:

- *This is a small, feathery bird.*
- *Some people hunt and eat these little birds.*

- *God gave his people these birds to eat when they were very hungry.*
- *The bird's name rhymes with "pail."*

After kids have identified the bird as a quail, say: **Quails are cute little birds, aren't they? They might be small, but they played a big part in God's provision for his people when Moses led the Hebrews out of slavery in Egypt! Quail begins with the letter Q, and today we'll discover how this little bird fed God's people in a big way. We'll also learn that God gives us what he knows we need. As we learn, let's make yummy quail salads to eat!** Hand each child a paper plate.

Quails roam freely in biblical lands and are only about seven inches long, so they can easily hide in tall grass. (Place lettuce leaves as pretend grass on the paper plates.) **Quails have brown feathers with white streaks in them and small reddish-colored eyes.** (Hand each child two raisin "eyes.") **Quails must fly long distances every winter and must stop to rest often. It's during these resting times that quail can be easily caught for their meat. When Moses led the Hebrews out of Egypt and into the wilderness, the hungry people grumbled. Say, how do your salads look? Are your ready to nibble your cool quails?**

Pause for kids to respond that they're missing the quails, then say: **Moses and God's people wanted quail, too—or at least *something* to eat! So Moses prayed and asked God to feed the people, and God answered by giving them manna, a sort of sticky bread, and plump quail.** Hand each child a portion of cold chicken breast to place on the lettuce leaves. Have kids add the raisins as eyes. Read aloud Exodus 16:12, 13, then ask:

- **Why was it smart for Moses to pray for God's help?**
- **How did God's answer to the people show his love?**

READING THE WORD

Before eating your salads, read 2 Peter 1:3. Say: **The people in Moses' time were thankful that God provided for their needs.**

- **How does God supply our needs?**
- **How can we thank God for giving us what we need?**

Say: **I'm so glad that God gives us what we need, aren't you? And a good way to thank God for his provision is through a prayer of thanksgiving! Let's share a prayer thanking God for supplying all we need to live!**

Share a prayer thanking God for providing for our needs. Add a dollop of mayonnaise for feathers, then enjoy nibbling your cool quail salads.

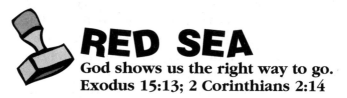

RED SEA

God shows us the right way to go.
Exodus 15:13; 2 Corinthians 2:14

A TO Z SUPPLIES: You'll need a Bible, saltwater and small drinking cups, self-sealing plastic sandwich bags, permanent markers, cornstarch, cooking oil, blue food coloring, water, measuring cups, permanent markers, and clear packing tape.
Before class, mix a small pitcher of saltwater.

SPELLING IT OUT

Gather kids and tell them you have a riddle. Tell kids the following riddle and see if they can guess what part of God's creation you're describing:

I go in and then go out—
I can't make up my mind!
I wave hello, then time to go,
I wave good-bye behind!

Say: **Now let me give you a tasty clue to the riddle!** Pour a bit of saltwater in each cup and let kids taste it. Then say: **The answer to our riddle is—the sea! The saltwater tastes like the seas God created, and one sea in the Old Testament was especially exciting! Even though we often think of seas and oceans being blue, this sea is called the Red Sea. It wasn't red in color but it was wet and deep and full of excitement for Moses and the Hebrew slaves who had just been set free from Pharaoh! Red Sea begins with the letter R, and today we'll learn how the Hebrew people learned that God always leads us in the right paths—even if those paths go through the middle of a sea!**

After God had freed the Hebrew slaves from Egypt, Moses followed God's directions and led the people away from the evil Egyptian pharaoh. But when Pharaoh came after the slaves, there was a big problem! Who remembers what that problem was?

Allow kids to retell how the Red Sea stood in the way of the Hebrews' escape. Continue: **Where could God's people go? What should they do? Follow God's paths, and he'd see them through! And God parted the waters for their amazing escape.** Ask:

- **What might have happened if the people hadn't followed God's leading?**
- **Why do you think God shows us the way to go?**
- **How is God's leading us a sign of his love and protection?**

READING THE WORD

Read aloud Exodus 15:13, then say: **Moses and God's people were in trouble, but Moses prayed and asked God to show them the way to go. And when God answered, the people obeyed and were saved. God is wiser than anyone and can show us the right way to go. All we have to do is obey him!** Ask volunteers to read aloud Proverbs 4:11-13 and 2 Corinthians 2:14. Then say: **I'm so glad that God shows us the right paths to take, but we need to remember to listen to God, then obey him to stay on those right paths—just as Moses did! Let's make seas-in-a-bag to remind us how God can part any troubles and show us the right way to go.**

Distribute the plastic bags and use permanent markers to write "Proverbs 4:11" on the bags. Then have kids each measure ¼ cup of cornstarch, ¼ cup of water, ¼ cup cooking oil, and three drops of blue food coloring in the plastic bags. Seal the bags tightly to remove excess air, then use clear packing tape to reinforce the seal. Tell kids to gently mix the cornstarch and liquids until they're dissolved and smooth. When you place the bags flat on a table and run your fingers over the bag, the "sea" will part!

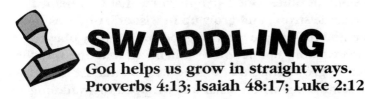

SWADDLING
God helps us grow in straight ways.
Proverbs 4:13; Isaiah 48:17; Luke 2:12

A TO Z SUPPLIES: You'll need a Bible, a baby blanket, a full-size blanket, scissors, self-adhesive hook and loop fasteners, and 1-inch-wide embroidered fabric trim.

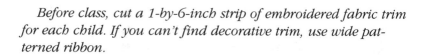

Before class, cut a 1-by-6-inch strip of embroidered fabric trim for each child. If you can't find decorative trim, use wide patterned ribbon.

SPELLING IT OUT

Hold up a baby blanket and ask kids what the blanket is typically used for. Encourage them to explain how to care for babies to make sure they grow up in good ways. Then say: **In Old Testament times, babies were wrapped—or swaddled—in blankets and strips of cloth. Today we'll discover what swaddling was and why people swaddled their babies. We'll also learn how God wants us to grow and how we can be swaddled in his love and truth.**

When babies were born in biblical days, their mothers would rub salt on their new skin because they believed it would make the baby's skin firm and smooth. After salting, the women wrapped the newborn in a square of cotton fabric, then wound strips of pretty cloth around the baby. Here, let's see what it was like to be swaddled!

Have a volunteer stand with hands at sides. Then have kids use the full-size blanket to wind the volunteer snuggly from one end of the blanket to the other, mummy-style (without covering the face). Say: **Can you move your arms easily? Probably not! Swaddling a baby kept its arms and legs straight and still—and this is how people believed babies grew in straight and strong ways! People believed that swaddling their babies would keep them warm and cozy and would also help their children grow in strong, straight ways.** Unwind the volunteer. If there's time, let each child be "swaddled" in the blanket.

READING THE WORD

Read aloud Proverbs 4:13 and Isaiah 48:17. Then say: **Even in Old Testament times, God's people knew that God helped them become strong and grow up in wisdom. God was the teacher, and his people grew in good ways if they obeyed God's instruction. But people also believed that one way for children to grow straight and good was to swaddle them as babies. Remember when Jesus was wrapped in swaddling cloths and laid in a manger?** Read aloud Luke 2:12.

Swaddling must have felt warm and snuggly, but it was God who helped Jesus grow in straight ways. We know that God wants us to grow in good, straight ways, too.

Some of these ways are through having faith in God, being truthful, learning God's Word, helping others, and being kind. These are all ways we grow up straight and strong for God. Ask:

- Why is growing in straight ways such as through honesty, love, and faith so important?
- Does our growing in these ways ever stop? Why?
- How can being "swaddled" in God's love and truth help us grow in good ways?

Say: **Let's make swaddling bracelets to remind us how we can be swaddled in God's love and truth to grow straight and strong!**

Show kids how to place a self-adhesive hook and loop fastener to one end of an embroidered fabric strip. Measure the strip so it fits snuggly, then add about a quarter inch and trim any excess fabric. Stick the other hook and loop fastener to the opposite side of the other end of the fabric as the other fastener.

Let kids wear their swaddling bracelets as you share a prayer thanking God for showing us good ways to grow straight and strong in his truth and love.

TENT

God covers us with his protection.
Psalms 91:1-4; 116:6; 145:20

A TO Z SUPPLIES: You'll need a Bible, a bedsheet or blanket, duct tape, construction paper, markers, clear tape, and glitter-glue pens.

Before class, plan an area where you and the kids can set up a "tent." You can construct a tent using a table or chairs and the bedsheet or by taping the sheet to the wall and floor to make an inside area large enough for kids to sit in.

SPELLING IT OUT

Place the duct tape and bedsheet or blanket on the floor in the center of the room and challenge kids to work cooperatively to construct a classroom tent. Give hints and helps as needed, but let.kids work together to accomplish the building.

When the tent is set up, have everyone gather inside, then say: **This is a great tent! Did you know that in Old Testament times many people lived all their lives in tents? The tents covered the people and protected them no matter where they decided to pitch them. Today we'll learn about tents and how God is like a loving tent to cover and protect us.**

Tents in Old Testament times were usually made of woven goat's hair, since it was so stiff and tough. They left the fabric its natural color, so the tents were striped in tan, brown, and black—just the color of goats! Tents usually had nine tent poles arranged in three rows of three poles each. The poles were close to six feet tall, so people could stand up in the tents. Inside, there were two rooms: one for sleeping and for entertaining company, and one that was separated off for the women's privacy. Ask:

■ **How did tents cover people and protect them?**
■ **In what ways does God protect us? cover us with love?**
■ **What would it be like to be out in the open with no protection? to be without God's protection and love?**

READING THE WORD

Say: **Tents were neat because no matter where people went, the tents could go along to cover and protect the people. That's just as it is with God! Wherever we go, God is always there caring for, protecting, and loving us!** Ask volunteers to read aloud Psalms 91:1-4; 116:6; and 145:20a. Then say: **God covers us with his protection because he loves us. God wants us to be safe and happy, and we can trust God to stay near and help us. Just as a tent covers and protects us from hot sunshine, storms, and cold, God covers and cares for us, too! So let's make table tents of our own to remind our families that wherever we are, God is covering us with his love!**

Show kids how to fold a sheet of construction paper into thirds, then decorate the six portions of the paper. Have kids write "God covers us" on one portion and questions about God's love or protection on the others. Use questions such as "How does God cover us?" and "When did you feel God's loving care today?" Tape the papers into triangular-shaped tents. Challenge kids to place their table tents on the dinner table and discuss a different question or God's covering grace with their families at each meal.

Close by going into your tent for a prayer. Pray: **Dear Lord, we thank you for covering us all the time with your wonderful love and protection. It makes us feel safe and loved to know you are covering us! We love you. Amen.**

UNLEAVENED
We can go when God calls!
Exodus 12:39; Luke 11:28

A TO Z SUPPLIES: You'll need a Bible, a slice of bread, flour tortillas, ¼ cup of orange juice, a cup of chopped walnuts, ¼ teaspoon of cinnamon, a bowl and spoon, plastic knives, and a pound of chopped, pitted dates.

Before class, boil the dates in 1½ cups of water for about ten minutes, then drain. You may wish to make copies of the recipe card from this object talk to send home with the kids.

SPELLING IT OUT

Gather kids and show them the slice of bread and the flat tortilla. Invite kids to tell the differences between the two, then say: **Both of these are types of bread, but one is made with yeast to make the bread fluffier and taller. This is called "leavened bread," and it takes a long time to prepare. Tortillas are an example of flat bread or "unleavened bread." U is for unleavened, and today we'll discover why God's people made unleavened bread and how, when God called them, they went!**

The Israelites had been slaves of Pharaoh for hundreds of years. This mean Egyptian king was cruel to them, so God sent Moses to set his people free. When God finally forced Pharaoh into freeing the Israelite slaves, they had to be ready to go in a hurry. There was no time to wait for bread to rise. So the Israelites made unleavened bread to take on their journey to freedom! Read aloud Exodus 12:39, then ask:

- Why was it important for the Israelites to go when God called?
- How did making unleavened bread help God's people "go for God"?
- How does being ready for God's calling help us to serve him?

READING THE WORD

Invite volunteers to read aloud Deuteronomy 27:10 and Luke 11:28. Ask:

- **In what ways can we prepare to obey and serve God when he calls?**
- **What might happen if we don't respond when God calls us?**
- **How does responding right away to God's commands show obedience and respect?**

Say: **The Israelites hurried when God called; they wanted to obey him at once. Their very lives depended on it, so they quickly made unleavened bread. Unleavened bread and a fruit spread called haroseth are still served today at Passover feasts to remind God's people to be ready to go for God when he calls!**

Let kids mix up a quick batch of haroseth. Have children help mix the dates, orange juice, chopped walnuts, and cinnamon in a bowl. Let each child take a turn adding an ingredient or stirring the mixture. When the haroseth is finished, let kids spread the treat on the flour tortillas.

Offer a prayer thanking God for helping us to be ready to respond to him with obedience and faith, then enjoy your treats!

HAROSETH & UNLEAVENED BREAD

You'll need ¼ cup of orange juice, a cup of chopped walnuts, ¼ teaspoon of cinnamon, flour tortillas, and a pound of chopped, pitted dates.

1. Boil the dates in 1½ cups of water for about 10 minutes, then drain.
2. Mix the dates, orange juice, chopped walnuts, and cinnamon in a bowl.
3. Spread the haroseth on flour tortillas and enjoy!

A B C D E F G H I J K L M

VINEYARD

God watches over us.
Psalms 1:6; 121:5; Isaiah 27:2, 3

A TO Z SUPPLIES: You'll need a Bible, a vine (real or artificial), grapes, green and purple construction paper, scissors, markers, tape, and brown-paper grocery sacks.

Before class, find a real vine to bring in or check for artificial vines in floral and craft departments. You may even have a grapevine wreath hanging in your home, and this would work well! You'll also need a small bunch of grapes for each child.

SPELLING IT OUT

Hold up the vine and ask kids what grows on a vine. Kids might suggest pumpkins, watermelons, grapes, and ivy. Tell kids you have a tasty clue as to what grows on the vines you will learn about today. Have kids close their eyes and open their mouths, then pop a grape into each expectant mouth. When kids guess that you'll be talking about grapes and vines, say: **Vines are mentioned often in the Bible, especially in relation to grapes and grapevines. Vineyards grew all over the lands of the Bible and were important to the people living there. Vineyard begins with the letter V, and today we'll discover why vineyards were important and mentioned so often in the Bible. We'll also learn that people back then watched over their vineyards just as God watches over us today.**

As early as Genesis 9:20, Noah was keeping a vineyard, and since that time grapes and vines have been important in biblical lands. Growing a good vineyard was hard work, and many animals and people might steal the grapes from off the vines. For this reason, small stone towers were built in vineyards. They were called "watchtowers" because farmers and their helpers stood in the towers to protect the vineyards. They wanted their vineyards healthy and whole because they were important in producing good fruit and grape drinks. Ask:

- How did protecting the vineyard show how much the farmer cared for the crops?
- In what ways does God's protection demonstrate his love for us?

READING THE WORD

Ask volunteers to read aloud Isaiah 27:2, 3 and Psalms 1:6; 121:5. Then say: **Vineyards were important to the people, so they protected them carefully. God protects us in much the same way. He watches over us and helps us if we're in trouble. Because God cares for and loves us so greatly, he watches over us.**

■ **How does it feel to know God is watching over you?**

■ **In what ways does God's caring love help us? strengthen our faith?**

Let's make neat grapevines that remind us of God's watchful, loving care. You can hang your vine in your bedroom or kitchen to read each day.

Have kids cut brown-paper grocery sacks into 6-inch-wide strips and tape the strips end to end to create a 3-foot-long strip. Then twist the brown paper to make snarly vines. Tear green-paper leaves and tape them to the vines. Then have each child cut out ten purple grapes and tape them into a bunch of grapes. Tape the grapes to the vine. Finally, challenge kids to write on their leaves ways that God watches over or protects us, such as through his love, through his Word, or through prayer.

End by sharing a prayer thanking God for watching over us in many ways. Have each child read one of the ways listed on her leaves, then end with a corporate "amen."

WASHING

We can honor and respect God.
Exodus 19:10; Matthew 22:37

A TO Z SUPPLIES: You'll need a Bible, a bar of soap, sawdust, olive oil, peppermint extract, measuring cups and spoons, and self-sealing plastic sandwich bags.

Before class, visit a woodworking shop, lumberyard, or building site to gather several cups of sawdust. You'll need a half cup of sawdust for each child. Kids will be mixing olive oil and sawdust to make a soap like the ancient Israelites used.

SPELLING IT OUT

Hold up the soap and ask kids to tell what soap is good for and what it cleans. Have kids explain why being clean is good and how it helps us stay healthy. Say: **Washing our bodies and clothes to keep them clean is important for many reasons. Today we know that dirt causes germs that can make us sick. So washing helps us stay healthy. But long ago people kept clean for another reason. Washing beings with the letter W, and today we'll learn why people in Old Testament times washed for God. We'll also discover that being clean is a wonderful way to honor and respect God even today!**

In Old Testament times, wearing clean clothes was a sign of respect when people worshiped God—and God demanded respect from his people. In fact, God told Moses that he would show himself to the people if they washed their clothes, which were dusty and dirty from their travels in the wilderness. Read aloud Exodus 19:10. **Another time, God's angel appeared before a priest named Joshua and told him to remove his filthy clothes—and Joshua obeyed** (Zechariah 3:3-5).

Of course, washing required soap. The Israelites made soap by mixing olive oil with powdered wood or plant ashes to make grits for scrubbing. It didn't smell very good, but it worked! Clothes were washed in streams or with well water and either beaten on rocks, stomped on, or whacked with sticks to make the dirt come loose. It took time to wash clothes, but the Israelites wanted to honor and respect God with their cleanliness. Ask:

- How can being clean show respect for God?
- In what other ways can we show respect for God?

READING THE WORD

Ask volunteers to read aloud Leviticus 16:30 and Matthew 22:37. Then say: **Respecting God means we obey him and love and honor him with all our hearts and minds. And it means we put God first in all we do, think, and say. Being clean in body and spirit allows us to feel good and healthy— just as God desires us to be. When we do the things God asks of us, we show respect and honor to him.** Ask:

- How does respecting and honoring God demonstrate our love for him?

Continue: **Let's make some super Israelite soap. When you use it to wash your hands, it will remind you of respecting and honoring God in all you do!**

Have each child measure ½ cup of sawdust, one tablespoon of olive oil, and several drops of peppermint extract or oil into a self-sealing sandwich bag. Seal the bags tightly, removing excess air, then gently mix the soap by kneading the ingredients. Tell kids to use a small amount of this unusual soap to clean their hands. Remind kids that Israelite soap didn't contain antibacterial ingredients, so only use the soap before or after washing with regular soap before meals. End by sharing a prayer telling God you want always to honor and respect him in all you do.

 # X-TRA SPECIAL
You're special in God's heart!
Psalms 37:28; 139:1-14

A TO Z SUPPLIES: You'll need a Bible, paper plates, bananas, powdered gelatin, plastic knives, permanent markers, and balloons.

Before class, inflate and tie off a balloon for each child in class. Write the child's name and "You're special!" on the balloon. Be sure you have a banana for every two kids. You'll also need extra balloons and bananas for another class, since your kids will be making treats to share with others. This object talk should have a party feel about it, since you will be "hosting" a You're Special party for your kids.

SPELLING IT OUT

Just before the talk, peel and cut bananas in half and place a half on each plate. Pour a small hill of powdered gelatin on each plate. Present a balloon as you hug each child and whisper "You're special to me!" Say: **I have special treats for you all today because I want to let you know you're special to me. As you enjoy your sparkly banana dips, we'll be discovering how "X-tra" special God thinks you are too! X is almost the beginning letter for the word** *extra,* **and God does think of each of you as extra special because he made you that way!**

The Bible tells us that, when God created the world, he saw that it was good. But God wanted someone to enjoy

the world and share in his creation. So God created people! The Bible tells us that God created people in his own
image. Neither plants nor animals nor rocks nor trees—
only people are in God's image! That's pretty special, isn't
it? And God gave each of us special abilities and talents,
likes and dislikes to make each of us unique. Ask:

- **What are some of the ways God made us special?**
- **How did God creating people in special ways show his
  love for us?**

When kids are finished with their treats, have them sit in the
center of the floor.

READING THE WORD

Read aloud Psalm 37:28 and take turns reading aloud 139:1-
14. Say: **You know, the Bible tells us that God loves us and I
know that is true. I know that is true because I *feel* loved
by God! I feel God's love in the way the world has so many
beautiful colors to enjoy and in the way God made flowers
and oceans and warm, fuzzy animals. And I also feel loved
and special because God stays with
me and wants to know what I think
and feel. How do you feel God's
love for you?** Allow time for kids to
respond. Continue: **It feels good
when someone thinks we're special. So let's make someone else
feel special by making them sparkly bananas and giving them balloons saying, "You're special to God!"**

Help kids prepare the treats and blow up the balloons. Write
"You're special to God!" on the balloons. Present your "party" to
the kids in another room and share with them a prayer thanking
God for making us special and for loving us.

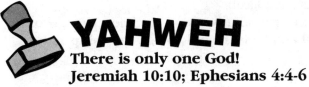

YAHWEH
There is only one God!
Jeremiah 10:10; Ephesians 4:4-6

A TO Z SUPPLIES: You'll need a Bible, poster board, colored markers, pencils, aluminum foil, and self-hardening clay.

Before class, write on poster board a list of the names of the children in your class. Someplace in the middle of the list, write the Hebrew word for "Yahweh," which is found in the margin. Place the list of names where kids can see it.

SPELLING IT OUT

Point to the list of names and ask kids to come and point to their names on the list as they say their names. When everyone has had a turn, read any names of kids who may be absent, then ask if kids can find any other names on the list. When the Hebrew word for Yahweh is pointed out, say: **That is a strange looking way to make letters, isn't it? But it *is* someone's name! Often we meet people who have the same names as ours, but there is only one who has this unusual name! I will tell you that this name is pronounced YAH-way and begins with the letter Y. Today we'll discover who Yahweh is and why there is only one name and one being who has this unusual name!**

The unusual name *Yahweh* is written in Hebrew on our list. Remember how we've learned that the Hebrews were God's people in the Old Testament? The Hebrews worshiped God, and they worshiped only one God—our God! God's name in Hebrew was Yahweh, but we don't know exactly what the name means. We do know it is from a Hebrew verb meaning "to be." But perhaps the name also means "one God," or perhaps Yahweh means something so wonderful we can't explain it! We refer to God as "God," but we have other names for him, too. What are some of the ways we call upon God?

Allow time for kids to tell that other names for God include Lord and Father, then tell kids that other names and ways to call upon God include Heavenly Father, Most High, and the God of Abraham, Isaac, and Jacob.

Say: **However we call upon God, we know there is only one true God and he is the only one we worship and praise!**

READING THE WORD

Invite volunteers to read aloud Jeremiah 10:10a; Mark 12:29; and Ephesians 4:4-6. Then ask:

A
B
C
D
E
F
G
H
I
J
K
L
M

- Why is it nice to have names that describe how wonderful God is?
- How can calling on God's name help us?
- How does it feel to know you worship and praise the only true God?

Say: **Some of the people we read of in the Old Testament were confused or downright awful because they chose to worship lots of false gods. Those people were foolish, weren't they? That's why Jesus told us in the New Testament to tell others about his love and God's saving grace, so that others would come to know, love, and follow the Lord just as we do! Let's make Yahweh paperweights to remind us who the only real God is—our God!**

Have kids make oval slabs with self-hardening clay. Be sure the slabs are about ½-inch thick. Use pencils to write the Hebrew tetragrammaton (Greek for "four letters") for Yahweh by using the pattern on your name list. Place the slabs on foil to take home. (The clay should harden in several hours.)

End with a prayer praising God as the only true God of our lives and thanking him for his love. Open your prayer with "Dear Heavenly Father" or even "Dear Yahweh."

ZITHER
There joy in praising God!
Psalms 33:1-3; 97:12; Romans 15:11

A TO Z SUPPLIES: You'll need a Bible, a musical instrument (real or toy), rubber bands, wrapping paper, tape, scissors, and a small box for each child.

Before class, collect a small, sturdy box for each child. Tissue boxes work well for this activity.

SPELLING IT OUT

Play your musical instrument for the kids and have them clap along with your creative "song." After a moment, stop in the middle of playing and say: **What a wonderful time to praise the Lord!** Continue playing for a few more moments, then set down your instrument. Invite kids to identify what their favorite musical instruments are or tell if they play a particular instrument. Say: **Music is a great way to express yourself! And in**

the Old Testament, music was the perfect way to express praise to God. One of the instruments used to praise God was called a zither. Zither beings with the letter Z, and today we'll learn what a zither is and how it was used to praise the Lord. We'll also discover that there's great joy in praising God.

Zithers were much like the small harps that people in Old Testament times played. Zithers were made from wood and had several strings to pluck, though the strings weren't made from string at all but from dried tendons of animal muscle. They were cut very thin and stretched tight in the hot sun to dry. Then the strings were oiled to keep them flexible and were strung tightly on the zither or harp. David loved playing the harp, and after he slew the mean giant Goliath, David played the harp for King Saul. David played a zither-like harp to praise God and tell God how wonderful he was! Ask:

- How do you think God feels when he hears our praises and worship?
- How does praising God show our love for him? Our joy in being loved by him?
- Why is it important to praise and honor God every day?

READING THE WORD

Have kids take turns reading aloud Psalms 33:1-3; 97:12; and Romans 15:11. Then say: **Praising God just with words makes me so happy, but when we add music there's even more joy! Let's express our joy and praise by making pretend zithers you can use to praise God every day.**

Have kids wrap the boxes using tape and gift wrap. Help kids cut a 3-inch hole in the center of the largest side of the box, then tape around the edges of the hole to keep the paper from tearing. Slide several rubber bands over the box so they lay across the hole. Invite kids to pluck their zithers as you read Psalm 33:1-3 again.

Finish by playing your zithers and having kids read aloud Psalm 150. End with a corporate "amen."